The School of Humility

Copyright ©2022 Ubong Orok Ekpenyong
All rights reserved. First paperback edition printed 2020 in the United Kingdom.
ISBN 978-1-913455-58-3
No part of this book shall be reproduced or transmitted in any form or by any means, electronic or mechanical, including photocopying, recording, or by any information retrieval system without prior written permission of the publisher.
Published by Scribblecity Publications.
Although every precaution has been taken in the preparation of this book, the publisher and author assume no responsibility for errors or omissions. Neither is any liability assumed for damages resulting from the use of this information contained herein.
Scripture quotations marked NLT are taken from the Holy Bible, New Living Translation, copyright © 1996, 2004, 2015 by Tyndale House Foundation. Used by permission of Tyndale House Publishers, Inc., Carol Stream, Illinois 60188. All rights reserved.

Dedication

To the Triune God: The Almighty God, my heavenly Father; Jesus Christ, my Lord and Saviour; the Holy Spirit, my comforter and counsellor.

I also dedicate this book to my dear husband, who has always been a great encourager and supporter, and to everyone who walks the path of humility.

CONTENTS

Acknowledgements	vii
Foreword	ix
Introduction	11
Chapter 1 Man is but Dust	13
Chapter 2 Pride Goes Before a Fall	21
Chapter 3 Learning Humility	42
Chapter 4 Humility Precedes Honour	48
Chapter 5 Test of Humility	56
Chapter 6 Heroes of Humility	63
Chapter 7 Language of Humility	89
Conclusion	97
References	98

Acknowledgements

My deepest appreciation goes firstly to Almighty God, the sustainer/giver of life and knowledge, by whose grace I am alive and was inspired to write this book.

Secondly, Jesus, my Saviour and Lord, through whose imputed righteousness I gained confidence to work on a topic bordering on humility that all mortals are striving to keep up with.

Thirdly, Holy Spirit, my comforter, who when I was downcast encouraged me not to abandon the work by strengthening me and keeping me on course to the successful completion of this work in good health. To the Triune God be all the glory and honour for the great things you have done!

Also, I seize this opportunity to acknowledge my dear husband, Sir (Engr) Orok, for standing by me from the beginning of this work to its completion. For all the time I deprived him of company while writing this book, he showed great understanding. When it was time for reviewing and editing, he painstakingly reviewed and edited the work.

Idee (my husband), what can I do without you! Thank you so much for your encouragement and believing in me that I could write this book. I love you beyond measure.

Furthermore, to all my children, "engrafted" children, and grandchildren, I say thank you for cheering me up and helping me realise the potential I have to achieve this goal. Odu, my son, you have been wonderful at typing the manuscript and also taking time to read through the work. This you did in record time, sparing me the stress I would have had doing that in a business centre.

I am grateful you did that for me in spite of your tight schedule at work and home. Thank you a million times over, son; you are always caring and supportive. I am so privileged to have you all: my husband, children, "engrafted" children, and grandchildren, in my life. The joy of having you here gave me strength to finish this book. What a blessed family given to me by God! Halleluyah! I love you all.

A special thanks to Pastor Samuel Olufemi Akinola, who, despite his crowded schedule, willingly accepted to write the foreword to this book. I am glad he did because, looking out for one fit to do this, I saw him as one with a humble disposition to approach. I thank you, sir, and also your dear wife, Dcns. Busola Akinola, for being longtime mentors to my husband and me.

Mrs Ubong Orok Ekenyong (Ph.D)

Foreword

Humility is one of the attributes of God. The word humility is a noun formed from humble. And it entails doing well while considering others better than yourself. The opposite of humility is pride.

Pride goes before a fall. Pride goes before destruction.

Humility is not backwardness. It does not look backward; it is forward-looking.

God and the Humble

It is natural to be loud and proud, but God
- Gives grace to the humble. 1 Pet. 5:5
- Gives more grace to the humble. Jas 4:6

David said in Psalms 9:1 "I will praise you, O Lord, with my whole heart, I will show forth all thy marvellous works."

In verse 12, King David, who is musically talented, said: "God does not forget the cry of the humble."

The Humble and the World

What we see more of in the world is people who are loud and proud of who they are and what they can do. This spirit has already entered the church.

Isaiah 57:15 reveals to us that God uses the spirit of the humble and contrite to revive the humble one.
It is a herculean task to write on such a subject as "The School of Humility." This is what Christians need to talk about more and more.

To you, my reader, please continue reading. You will be glad and grateful that you read the material. Get a copy for yourself and encourage someone else to read it.

Thank you Sister Ekpenyong, for the grace in your life to write. This gift is great. Thank you.

Remain blessed.

Pastor Samuel Olufemi Akinola
General Superintendent
(Glorious Covenant Ministry)

INTRODUCTION

The School of Humility is a school nobody wants to voluntarily enrol in. However, whether one likes it or not, it is a school all must pass through in order to be who God wants them to be.

There is no doubt human beings parade the world with the air of being in absolute control of their lives. How man's memory has failed him to know, like Job, that naked he came to this world and naked will he return (Job 1:21). We came to this world with nothing: no clothes, education, riches, positions, or fame. This notwithstanding, man is full of himself, though empty, because of his innate tendency towards pride. Addressing this innate tendency in man is better done in the school of humility.

Whereas in a formal school, one is taught by teachers in a classroom, in the school of humility, life itself is the teacher through the different circumstances of life we encounter. Here, one is forced to submit to the sovereignty of God and accept that nothing else matters but God.

As pride is swallowed up by humility, every student is guided by the school motto: "He that is down need fear no fall". Having the motto of the school in mind makes the journey through life rewarding as you end up on the honour roll having won the prizes of riches, wisdom, and long life.

However, if by reason of your achievements, wealth, and fame, you find it difficult to live by this motto and lie low in life, then this book—The School of Humility—is for you. Reading through the book, you will discover reasons you need to humble yourself before God and your fellow men.

Failure to see these reasons will make your journey through life painful, frustrating, and finally end in utter disgrace because whatever goes up must surely come down—where, you can't really tell. May you end well in life as you choose to follow the path of humility—the way those who you will read about in this book did and ended well in Jesus' name.

1
MAN IS BUT DUST

We are nothing but dust according to Psalm 103: 14-16 (NLT): *For He knows how weak we are; He remembers we are dust. Our days on earth are like grass; wind blows, we are gone- as though we had never been here.*

One would have expected the above Bible passage to have a humbling effect on man, but the reverse is the case. However, the regenerated—those who have given their lives to Jesus Christ—have the understanding that they are nothing but dust, as reflected in their lives' humble disposition. Others who live in the flesh and are unregenerated are full of themselves. At the slightest provocation, you hear such people make statements like, Do you know who I am? They think so highly of themselves, not having the slightest inkling that life is brief and

likened to:
- Grass
- Flower
- Vapour

Grass

The greenness of grass is so refreshing to a man's spirit, soul, and body. Green depicts life, and this makes it a valuable commodity. Those who value nature (including my husband and I) will do everything to ensure that the grass in their environment is well nurtured, including mowing and watering it at all times.

This is what they do because they fully understand the characteristics of grass. The same grass that blossoms and stays green when pruned and watered withers, dies, and dries up when no care is given to it. What once made the environment beautiful and lively is eventually raked away, for it is no longer green and beautiful to behold.

Similarly, where man does not abide in Christ—his or her source of life—he or she is cut off and will lose relevance in life, irrespective of who he or she claimed to be. The lesson here for all is that, as grass amounts to nothing for lack of care by man, so will man be if he/she refuses to owe everything he/she has to God—his/her caretaker and helper.

According to 1 Peter 1:24-25b (KJV):
For all flesh is as grass, and all the glory of man as the flower of grass. The grass withereth and the flower thereof away. But the word of the Lord endureth forever.

Flower
Each flower, like a human being, has its own unique signature, qualities, and beauty. In comparing man with a flower, the word of God reveals their similarity, with the beauty of a flower surpassing that of a man.

Man born of a woman is of few days and full of trouble. He springs up like a flower and withers away like a fleeting shadow, he does not endure (Job 14:1-2 NIV).

And why should you be anxious about clothes? Consider the lilies of the field and learn thoroughly how they grow; they neither toil nor spin. Yet

> *I tell you, even Solomon in all his magnificence (excellence, dignity, and grace) was not arrayed like one of these* (Matthew 6:28-29 AMP).

The main purpose of clothing is to cover one's nakedness and keep one warm from the cold. But people have long changed that purpose to that of affluence, i.e., self-arrival, as the perceived flamboyantly dressed people take pride in their clothing. As a result, those who lack beautiful clothing feel less important and become worried. It is vanity and foolishness on the part of those who indulge in such acts, for even the splendid clothing of King Solomon, as recorded in the Bible, was no match for the beauty of flowers. Of a truth, watching arrays of natural flowers in gardens, on the streets, and in shops is breath-taking—the reason I love flowers so much. As one who grows plants and tends them, I watch them with keen interest. Watching them as they grow is so refreshing that I wish they could last forever. But when their season is over, I observe that they wither and suddenly fade away and die. Such is the life of a man who comes up in full vigour, rejoicing in his youth, strength, beauty, achievements, and fame in his season. Then, suddenly, at the appointed time set by

God, there is no more strength and stability in him or her to prowl around proudly. In no distant time, he or she dries up, fades away, and dies, returning to the dust that he or she is.

Lesson for all

Learn not to glory in yourself but in God alone. Like a flower that blossoms, withers, fades away, and dies, so you will fade away and die, disappearing into the thin air of oblivion.

Vapour

Life is a vapour, one reason being that it is frail and short-lived. You see the mist at one moment, and a few minutes later, it's gone. You see steam coming out of your tea cup, and in just a second, it disappears into the air. Life is just like that. Even if you are to live for 100 years, before you know it, as time flies quickly by, you are there and gone. Like a roll of toilet paper, the closer you get to the end, the quicker it goes! You may not take this analogy seriously, but it's true! Even as Psalm 90:10 (NLT) alludes to:

> *Seventy years are given to us! Some even live to eighty. But even the best years are filled with pain*

and trouble; soon they disappear, and we fly away.

How then should we live our lives in view of the fact that life is a vapour? That God is sovereign? That we are prone to pride?

1. We should live praying the prayer in Psalm 90:12 (NLT) always: *Teach us to realise the brevity of life so that we may grow in wisdom.*
Only God can give you the wisdom you need to live your life profitably with eternity in view.

2. Accept that death is certain as pointed out in Heb.9:27 (NLT): *And just as each person is destined to die once and after that come judgement.*

My husband and I once had the shock of our lives in the 80s when we went to visit one of our family friends who had retired from service to his country home. We went to see him and share fellowship with him, but alas, he had died unknown to us. All we could see was his grave, an affirmation that life is a vapour. That notwithstanding, people carry on in life as if they will live forever, not believing they can die at any moment. The certainty of death should make every person desperate to know how to get right with God. Trusting God is the only true source of security for the future. In the book of James 4:14, we see that life is a vapour and that God is sovereign over every aspect of life.

3. Shun pride for this is a great sin that easily plagues us all. Talk not proudly for man can only propose and never dispose. According to James 4:13-16, never you say: *"Today or tomorrow, I'll go to a certain town to do business and make profit for you know not what your life will be like tomorrow"*. Only God can dispose, so always add *"by the grace of God or God willing"* whenever you make any proposal. Had Napoleon Bonaparte, the French military genius known that, he would not have met his downfall when he did. He went all out to invade Russia against his friend's dissuasion. Even when the friend told him that men propose but God disposes, he snapped back "I propose as well as dispose". What impunity! God will not allow any man to usurp his prerogative with impunity. Sure enough, Napoleon's invasion of Russia was the beginning of his downfall. Considering the fact that life is a vapour and pride a constant battle to fight, the only sane course to follow with eternity in view is humble obedience to God's will.

What is God's will for your life? Mine is to glorify God as a godly wife, mother, and grandmother, using my talent and God-given wealth to build up His church and further the gospel for the expansion of His kingdom on earth.

Lesson for all:

Take God into consideration in all your planning and always let your will be melted into His in all you do. Failure to do this is pride, which is a sin that can lead to one's destruction unexpectedly.

CHAPTER 2

PRIDE GOES BEFORE A FALL

It is very rare to come across a person who publicly claims he or she is proud. People express their pride through their words, carriage, and actions. A deep search into the meaning of pride is required when people claim to be humble but still manifest pride in their lives.

Pride is a feeling of deep pleasure or satisfaction derived from one's own achievements, the achievements of those with whom one is closely associated with or from qualities or possessions that are widely admired. [1]

According to the Merriam-Webster dictionary, pride is the quality or state of being proud, such as inordinate self-esteem, a reasonable or justifiable sense of self-respect, or delight or elation arising from some act, possession, or relationship with cause for parental pride.

---

1   *Oxford Advanced Learner's Dictionary*, 9th edition

From the definitions above, the feeling of deep pleasure or satisfaction gotten from your achievements or the achievements of your close associates is not bad. But having a too high opinion of yourself or your abilities, feeling you are better or more important than other people, and failing to acknowledge the supremacy and excellency of the Almighty God (the Maker of all things) in all you are, do, or have at all times is bad and seen as pride.

Basically, pride is sin, which refers to a high or exalted attitude—the opposite of humility, which is the appropriate posture people ought to have with God and man. Of all the things listed in Proverbs 6:16-19 (AMP) that God detests, pride tops the list:

> *These six things the Lord hates, indeed, seven are an abomination to Him: A proud look (the spirit that makes one overestimate himself and underestimate others) a lying tongue, and hands that shed innocent blood, A heart that manufacture wicked thoughts and plans, feet that are swift in running to evil, A false witness who breathes out lies (even under oath), and he who sows discord among his brethren.*

The day you harbour pride in your life, you become the enemy of God, awaiting your fall like a pack of cards. A proud person must surely fall for whatever goes up must come down. Besides, God resists the proud but gives grace to the humble (James 4:6).

When God withdraws his grace from you, you are left with nothing but disgrace and impending destruction when you choose not to repent. The truth cannot be compromised; pride goes before a fall (Proverbs 16:18). This can be seen in the lives of Nebuchadnezzar, King Herod, Goliath, and Haman, to name just a few Biblical examples of people who exalted themselves above their fellow human beings and even God. We will examine how each was destroyed by pride.

Nebuchadnezzar

King Nebuchadnezzar II was one of the most powerful rulers ever to appear on the world stage. He reigned in the Neo-Babylonian Empire (605 BC–562 BC). He was regarded as the greatest and most powerful ruler, with a formidable military force. Yet like all other kings, his might was nothing in the face of the Almighty God, the Maker of all things and the God of the Angelic Armies, to whom all power, wisdom, honour, and glory belong.

Nebuchadnezzar is best known as the Babylonian King who destroyed and conquered Jerusalem in 586 BC, leading many Hebrews, including Daniel, Shadrach, Meshach, and Abednego, into captivity in Babylon.

He became an incredibly successful conqueror and builder—the reason why many bricks have been found in Iraq (Babylon) with his name stamped on them. He gained stature as a military commander by defeating the Egyptians under Pharaoh at the battle of Carchemish (2 Kings 24:7; 2 Chronicles 35:20; Jer. 46:2).

During his reign, he greatly expanded the Babylonian Empire. He undertook the rebuilding and beautification of his home town and the capital city of Babylon. The hanging gardens of Babylon, one of his architectural achievements, rank among the seven wonders of the ancient world. He was indeed an able but ruthless ruler who let nothing get in his way of subduing people and conquering lands.

What a great king he was, but his undoing was pride. Had he known that pride goes before a fall, he would have lived his life differently. He would not have allowed himself to be easily manipulated and imagined he was equal with God by desiring worship. Not realising he was merely an instrument in God's hand to shape world history in his time, he resorted to boasting in Dan. 4:30 (NLT), and verse 25 clearly states the Most High rules in the kingdom of men and gives it to whomever He chooses.

> *As he looked out across the city, he said, "look at this great city of Babylon! By my own mighty power, I have built this beautiful city as my royal residence to display my majestic splendour."*

The statement above earned King Nebuchadnezzar more than enough credentials for admission to the school of humility. That statement made in arrogance, boastfulness, and effrontery provoked God to humble a dignified king by turning him into a wild beast. For seven years, he lived the life of a beast in the forest— the school where he learned humility. No doubt, he acknowledged the sovereignty of God when his senses returned to him, as recorded in Daniel 4:34–37 (NLT):

> *After this time had passed, I Nebuchadnezzar looked up to heaven. My sanity returned, and I praised and worshiped the Most High and honoured the one who lives forever.*
> *His rule is everlasting and His kingdom is*

everlasting. All the people of the earth are nothing compared to Him. He does as he pleases among the angels of heaven and among the people of the earth. No one can stop Him or say to Him, What do you mean by doing these things?

When my sanity returned to me, so did my honour and glory and Kingdom. My advisers and nobles sought me out and I was restored as head of my Kingdom, with even greater honour than before. Now, I Nebuchadnezzar praise and glorify and honour the king of heaven. All His acts are just and true, and he is able to humble the proud.

Are you like Nebuchadnezzar, who before he learned humility thought his achievements came from his own efforts? Remember, it is only by the mercy and grace of God that we succeed in all of our endeavours and reach lofty heights.

If, by the grace of God, we amount to what we are, should we glory in ourselves? Absolutely, no man on earth should give glory to himself. All the glory must be given to God, who makes all things possible.

Lessons for all:

1. Humility and obedience to God matter more than worldly achievements.
2. No matter how mighty a man may become, God's power is greater. Nebuchadnezzar conquered nations but was helpless in the hands of the Almighty God. God controls the rich and the powerful to carry out his plans.
3. Daniel had watched kings come and go, including Nebuchadnezzar. He understood that only God should be worshipped for He alone holds sovereign power and so also should you.

King Herod

The writings of Solomon say: *Pride goes before destruction, a haughty spirit before a fall* (Proverbs 16:18), and this played out in the life of King Herod Agrippa I in a very dreadful manner. Herod Agrippa was the grandson of King Herod, who had attempted to kill Jesus as a baby. He was just as bloodthirsty as his grandfather, being responsible for the death of James. But for God, Peter would have been killed too.

King Herod Agrippa was a powerful and very proud man. He had exerted his power to the point that the cities of Tyre and Sidon, two cities that had been in dispute with him, humbled themselves and sought to make peace with him. As he sat before them making a speech, they shouted out, *It is the voice of God and not of man* (Acts 12:22 NLT). Because Herod revelled in this praise and did not give God the glory, an angel of the Lord struck him, and instantly his body decayed and was infested with worms that ate him up to death.

If there is one thing God hates, it is pride, as Proverbs 16:5 clearly states he detests the proud. Amongst the reasons is because pride places a wall between us and Him. Pride makes us think we do not need God and can live without Him. Our pride also puts a barrier between us and others. How often, because of our pride, do we destroy our relationships, friendships, marriages, and families? And as with Herod, pride will ultimately lead to our destruction if we refuse to repent.

If we, in our pride, say, "I don't need you, God", He will eventually give us what we want—life for all eternity without Him—only to suddenly realise that we are cut off from life, love, joy, and peace, as all of these things find their source in God. This is what Herod found out. What about you? Is your pride standing between you and your spouse, the people at work, or at church? Even worse, is it standing between you and God? Ponder over what Peter says in 1 Peter 5:5b–6 (NIV):

God opposes the proud but gives grace to the humble. Humble yourselves, therefore, under God's mighty hand, that he may lift you up in due time.

Lessons for all:

1. Never speak so arrogantly whenever you have an opportunity to make an oration. Address your audience in humility and when applauded or given standing ovation, do not be puffed up but be quick to return all the glory to God. Herod failed to do this and incurred the wrath of God instantly, for His glory He will not share with any man.

2. Whenever people praise you for your achievement in any sphere of life, tell them it is all the Lord's doing and not by your soul effort; for without God, you can do nothing (Jn.15:5). If then you can do nothing of your own, there is no reason to act proudly in the face of any achievement.

3. Remember there is nothing you achieve today that people already have not achieved. Moreover, come tomorrow, many more people will surpass you in their success stories. Boast and glory only in the Lord.

Goliath

Goliath was a Philistine war champion from Gath, who by reason of his height and military skill became so proud and resorted to boasting as he challenged Israel's army to fight. For forty days every morning and evening, he strutted in front of the Israelite army taunting in 1 Sam.17:8-10 (NLT):

> *Why are you all coming out to fight? He called, I am the philistine champion, but you are only the servant of Saul. Choose one man to come down here and fight me! If he kills me, then we will be your slaves! But if I kill him, you will be our slaves! I defy the armies of Israel today! Send me a man who will fight me!*

What could have made Goliath talk this way? Could it be his mindset? I guess his thought pattern was: "I am the greatest; I am the most secure; I can fight and beat anyone; this will be no contest at all! It is a walk-over fight for me". Drawing interference from this mindset, Goliath must have felt he did not need God or even the Philistine army to help him as he considered himself able to solve all his problems. Many of us are like Goliath when it comes to thinking more highly of ourselves than we ought to. Mohammed Ali, who claimed to be the greatest in the days of his boxing career, was a man in the evening of his life who needed to be supported to walk or raise his hand! In fact, boasting is an exercise in futility as it borders on pride, the sin God so much detests.

He resists the proud and withdraws His grace from such a person, to his or her detriment. Had Goliath known this, he would not have disdained young David, a man after God's own heart, who showed up to fight him with just five smooth stones, a sling, and a shepherd's staff. Sneering at him in contempt, Goliath yelled in 1 Sam. 17:43-44 (NLT):

Am I a dog, he roared at David, that you come at me with a stick? He cursed David by the names of his gods. Come over here, and I will give your flesh to the birds and wild animals!

David however replied in 1 Sam.17:43-44(NLT):

You come to me with sword, spear, and javelin, but I come to you in the name of the Lord of Heaven's Armies- the God of the armies of Israel, whom you have defied. Today the Lord will conquer you and cut off your head. And I will give the dead bodies of your men to the birds and wild animals and the whole world will know that the Lord rescues his people, but not with sword and spear. This is the Lord's battle and he will give you to us!

Quite unexpectedly for Goliath and his men, the fight took a different turn as David, armed with the inferior weapons of a shepherd but empowered by God, killed the "mighty" Goliath. Halleluiah! No one can battle with the Lord. Two scriptures readily come to mind here: It is not of him that runneth or willeth but of God that showeth mercy" (Rom. 9:16 KJV). *Not by might nor by power, but by my spirit, says the Lord Almighty* (Zechariah 4:6 KJV).

Therefore, stop thinking you are the greatest, as this is the preserve of God. Whenever we set out to do anything, we should always remember that our power, intellect, expertise, and resources will certainly fail us if we do not trust God to help us. Our ways are not His ways, and our thoughts are not His thoughts. Goliath, who defied God and trusted in his might, war expertise, and gods, lost the battle to David, who trusted in the Almighty God to give him victory.

Lesson for all:
If anybody desires to be great, let such a person seek and acknowledge God, the source of greatness as David did.

Haman

The Bible, in the book of Esther, 3:1 presents Haman as a man who was an official in the court of the Persian Empire under king Ahasuerus, commonly identified as Xerxes. He was an Agagite, the son of Hammedatha. He was likely a descendant of Agag, king of the Amalekites, longtime enemies of the Jewish people. With pride added to his resume, probably because he considered himself a prince, he stands out as a vivid case study of the statement in Proverbs 16:18 (KJV): *Pride goeth before destruction, and an haughty spirit before a fall.*

Going through the pride stories of Haman and others who let pride rage unchecked, the statement above cannot be refuted. Pride makes us build ourselves up. Instead of encouraging other people, we pull them down in order to feel better than them, as played out in Haman's life.

There was a time in Shushan's palace when two of the king's chamberlains, Bigthan and Teresh, plotted to assassinate the king (Esther 2:21–23). Fortunately, the plot was unravelled by Mordecai, a Jew who sat in the king's gate, and the matter was recorded in the Book of the History of King Xerxes' Reign. After investigation of the matter, the two assassination plotters were killed, and Haman was promoted over all other nobles. Why Haman and not Mordecai? I perceive that the proud Haman must have painted the picture that he worked hard to save the king's life, propelling the king to make him the most powerful official in the empire.

In addition, the king commanded all his officials to bow down before Haman to show him respect whenever he passed by. All the palace officials complied with the order except Mordecai, who I think must have believed only God should be bowed down to and worshipped. As a result, Haman left his rage unchecked and decided to kill Mordecai, as well as all other Jews in the entire empire of Xerxes, having learned of Mordecai's nationality. Oh, what a terrible thing it is for one to harbour the monster called pride and allow it to hold sway in his or her life.

Pride makes us build ourselves up. Instead of encouraging other people, we pull them down in order to feel better than them, as played out by Haman, who tried all he could to destroy Mordecai and all other Jews just because Mordecai refused to bow to him. Haman went to the extent of convincing the king to issue a decree that they be destroyed, which the king did and confirmed by removing his signet ring from his finger and giving it to him. Esther 3:8-10 (NLT) records:

> *Then Haman approached king Xerxes and said, "There is a certain race of people scattered through all the provinces of your empire who keep themselves separate from everyone else. Their laws are different from those of any other people, and they refuse to obey the laws of the king. So it is not in the King's interest to let them live. If it pleases the king, issue a decree that they be destroyed, and I will give 10, 000 large sacks of silver to the government administrators to be deposited in the royal treasury". The king agreed, confirming his decision by removing his signet ring from his finger and giving it to Haman son of Hammedatha the Agagite, the enemy of the Jews.*

What Haman failed to know in building himself up is that our thoughts are not God's thoughts and our ways are not His ways (Isa. 55:8).

Haman thought Mordecai was a nobody—a mere gatekeeper and a Jew—to be taught a lesson he would not live to tell. Unknown to him, he was putting his own life on the line because he was opposing not just the cousin of Queen Esther but also the wife of King Xerxes, his boss.

In fact, things took a different turn when Esther got a copy of the decree to annihilate all the Jews. She was determined to go to the King to make a petition for her people at the expense of her life, for it was not yet time for her to appear before the King in his inner court. However, after fasting with her people for three days, she went in to see the king. God granted her favour, with the king ready to give her even up to half of the kingdom, as *the king's heart is in the hand of the Lord, as rivers of water: He turneth it whithersoever he will* (Prov. 21:1 KJV).

Esther's request for the king and Haman to come to the banquet she prepared for them was granted on two occasions. After the first banquet, there was another invitation to a second banquet to enable Esther to make her petition known to the king. Wow! This was mindblowing for the proud Haman, reading from Esther 5:9-10(KJV):

Then went Haman forth that day joyful with a glad heart: but when Haman saw Mordecai in the king's gate, that he stood not up, nor moved for him, he was full of indignation against Mordecai.

Nevertheless Haman refrained himself: and when he came home, he sent and called for his friends, and Zeresh his wife.

Even though Haman basked in self-glorification, he was not himself each time he saw Mordecai at the gate not bowing to him; he considered all his achievements and honour worthless. Remember, until a proud person pulls down other people to build himself, he or she will let nothing or anyone stand in his or her way to being the greatest, as in the case of Haman in Esther 5:11-13 (KJV):

And Haman told them of the glory of his riches, and the multitude of his children, and all the things wherein the king had promoted him, and how he had advanced him above the princes and servants of the king. Haman said moreover, Yea,

> *Esther the queen did let no man come in with the king unto the banquet that she had prepared but myself; and tomorrow am I invited unto her also with the king. Yet all this availeth me nothing, so long as I see Mordecai the Jew sitting at the king's gate.*

Subsequently, Haman bought the idea from his wife and all his friends to hang Mordecai on the gallows already set up. Nevertheless! Our ways are not God's ways. The night before the day Haman planned to hang Mordecai, the king could not sleep, and therefore he ordered that the book of records of history in his reign be read to him. There, it was found out that Mordecai had unravelled the plot to kill the king, and nothing was done to reward him. Meanwhile, Haman came shortly after to ask the king to hang Mordecai on the gallows that had been prepared for him. Before he could make his request, the king asked him what could be done to the man he was delighted to honour. Very typical of a proud man's thinking: "Who else but me would the king delight to honour?" Haman thought and quickly gave his counsel that such a man should be dressed in royal apparel and led on horseback in a procession through the streets of the city with the proclamation, *Thus shall it be done to the man whom the king delighted to honour* (Esther 6:8-9 KJV).

Haman gave the above counsel because a proud man thinks no other person can be better than himself. To his greatest amazement, the king asked him to do as he had said to Mordecai, the Jew, and the gateman at the palace gate. With such a detailed description, I perceive the king did not want him to make a mistake as there could be another Mordecai. He had no choice but to obey the king's command. After riding Mordecai on a horse back through the streets of the city and dropping him at the king's gate, Haman went home to his house in a hurry, having his head covered and mourning. Truly, God resists the proud but gives grace to the humble. Honouring Mordecai instead of hanging him was so humiliating for Haman. But this was only the beginning of his downfall.

On the day of Esther's second banquet with the king and Haman, things went awry for Haman as Esther revealed his evil plan against the Jews (to have them all destroyed). Seeing the king was very angry with him, Haman fell on the bed where Esther sat to plead with her to make a request for his life. To the king, Haman's falling on the bed to plead with Esther meant he wanted to rape his wife right before him. As the king spoke up, Haman's face was covered, and he was taken out and hanged on the gallows he had prepared for Mordecai as directed by the king. How true is the statement in Proverbs 16:18 (KJV): "Pride goeth before destruction, and a haughty spirit before a fall"?.

There is absolutely nothing that should make us proud. Is it your beauty? Remember, there are many good-looking people who can beat you in any beauty contest. Your smooth skin, which makes you beautiful today, will wax old with time, and you will be left with wrinkles and nothing more to be proud of. Or is it your educational qualification? No matter the number of degrees you have, a time will come when your knowledge will become obsolete because knowledge is always increasing and dynamic. If it is wealth, no matter how much money you have, you cannot own everything you want at the same time.

You will always see somebody who is richer than you with what you cannot afford at the time you want. In line with the above, we all ought to swallow our pride in every area of our lives and rather resolve to boast in the

Lord alone, who gives us life that no money can buy. Through God alone comes every good and perfect gift (James 1:17).

Lessons for all:
1. No condition in life is permanent. Everything is temporal and transient, even life itself in the physical.
2. Feeling good at the expense of regarding everyone as inferior to you comes from your feeling of insecurity.
3. When you have God, you have everything and will always feel secure, valuing other people more than yourself.

CHAPTER 3
LEARNING HUMILITY

While writing the introduction to this book, I made mention of pride as an innate human tendency. What this means is that pride is inborn or natural. Every human being is born with some element of pride in order to grow up with good self-worth or esteem, without which an inferiority complex seems inevitable. Unfortunately, some people allow their pride to develop to the point where they now have a too high opinion of themselves, feeling they are better than other people. In such a scenario, learning humility to check such pride is imperative.

According to the Oxford Dictionary, humility is the quality of having a modest or low view of one's own importance. Unlike pride, which is inherent, we become humble by learning that we know little and accepting who we are, where we are, and where we are going. Humility is actually being honest with ourselves.

What is learning? According to the dictionary definition, it is the acquisition of knowledge or skills through study, experience, or being taught. In the field of education, it is believed learning occurs only when there is a change in behaviour as a result of one's study or experience for better performance in future learning.

The best way to learn anything is by example. When teachers give their pupils or students examples while they teach, the topics are easily understood by them. Following the examples, they imbibe the lessons and are able to solve similar problems subsequently. In a similar vein, humility can be learned through life's circumstances, ranging from incurable sickness, major financial loss, and a terrible accident, just to mention a few. There is no circumstance from which we cannot learn humility if we maintain the right attitude, for we change only when our fear is surpassed by our pain.

However, we do not have to wait until major problems come into our lives to humble us by force. We should follow the example of our Lord Jesus Christ who humbled himself and died a shameful death on the cross just to reconcile us back to God. Following Christ's example is possible only if we have the mind of Christ as stated in Phil.2: 6-8 (NLT):

Though he was God, he did not think of equality with God as something to cling to instead, he gave up his divine privileges; he took the humble position of a slave and was born as a human being. When he appeared in human form, he humbled himself in obedience to God and died a criminal's death on the Cross.

Do you have the mind of Christ? It takes repentance from sin and surrendering your life to Him to have His mind. If you are not in Christ, you will not have this mind. That means you have a mind of your own, live for yourself, and are easily puffed up to cover an inferiority complex. As a matter of fact, learning humility for a person who is not in Christ usually comes by force through unpleasant circumstances. If you are in doubt, the story of Nebuchadnezzar, who for seven (7) years learned humility in the forest under rain and sun in the midst of wild animals, is there for you to read (Dan. 4:33–35). Really, it is only when you realise who you are, where you are, and where you are going that you can learn humility.

Who are You?

You are created by God in His image according to Genesis 1:27. This means you were created as God's representative ruler, having dominion over every other creation of God. Did you know that? David knew this so well that he had this to say in Psalm 139:14 (KJV): I will praise thee; for I am fearfully and wonderfully made: Marvellous are thy works; and that my soul knoweth right well.

Even though you were born royal in the light of the above scripture, you came into this world naked as rightly stated by Job in Job 1:21. This points to one fact- you came into the world with nothing. Therefore, in all your gettings and achievements, maintain a humble disposition and return all the glory to God who made your success story possible. Without God, we are nothing. But through the knowledge of Christ, God has given us all things that pertain to life and godliness (2 Pet. 1:3). So, see yourself as special and bid the inferiority complex farewell, for only when we count ourselves as special and blessed people can we practise humility.

Where are You?

Your position in Christ will determine how much humility you can learn. Humility is a virtue you receive when you give your life to Christ. Are you in Christ?

If you are, you will not struggle with learning humility because the Holy Spirit, in whose fruit humility is found (Gal. 5:22–23), will help you as you develop intimacy with Christ. Galatians 2:20 states that Christ lives in us and not our old selves or natures, which have been crucified with Him.

In Christ you discover that you are a joint heir with him. As a result, in any situation you find yourself in—good or bad—you maintain a good sense of self-worth and a humble disposition.

Unfortunately, many who are not in Christ are yet to come to terms with the above. Based on the circumstances they find themselves in, they develop poor self-worth, feel so insecure that they compensate by acting superior.

Where are You Going?

Hebrews 9:27 tells us that it is appointed unto every man once to die, and after that judgement. Even if you have to live for 200 years on earth, death is imminent. If certainly you will one day die, remember one sin God detests so much is pride. Do you want to go and meet God as a proud man? Don't you think He will resist you and judge you rightly?

Also, remember that just as you came into the world with nothing, you are leaving it with nothing. Therefore, there is no need to take pride in anything we own or achieve in this world. Everything you have worked for and acquired can one day develop wings and fly away. Solomon, who saw the best and worst of life, said everything is meaningless in Eccl.1:2 (KJV):
Vanity of vanities, saith the preacher, vanity of vanities; all is vanity.

Nevertheless, if you have Jesus as your Lord and Saviour, you will find life meaningful, for the joy and peace He gives are enough to make you walk on stormy seas while you are alive. Even at death, eternal life in joy and peace awaits you.

CHAPTER 4

HUMILITY PRECEDES HONOUR

In a world where everyone wants to be held in high esteem and given special recognition, humility is one attribute that is much to be desired by all. It is pertinent to note that humility and honour always go together. Whenever you see humility, expect to see honour come after, all things being equal. As a matter of fact everybody wants to be honoured, but very few people have actually taken the proper steps to be placed in the seat of honour. 1 Peter 5:6 (KJV) says: "Humble yourself therefore under the mighty hand of God, that He may exalt you in due time".

The first step to take towards the place of honour is that of humility, as stated above. In humbling yourself before God, you are submitting to Him, honouring Him, and seeing Him as the one in charge and not you. As a result, He will honour you, because for those that honour Him, He will honour; and for those that despise Him, He will lightly esteem (1 Sam.2:30b).

By the way, what is humility? Recall that it is the quality or state of being humble—not thinking you are better than other people.

Sadly, many of us lack this quality and that has robbed us of many opportunities that would have taken us to the next level of our lives—the place of honour.

What then is honour? Honour can be defined as high respect that is given to someone who is admired for his or her good reputation, good quality, or character (high moral standards of behaviour) as judged by other people. For you to be adjudged a man or woman of honour, it takes high moral standards of behaviour, which can only be made possible by God as one submits to him. Otherwise, you will be seen as a man or woman of dishonour, for God resists the proud and gives grace to the humble (1 Pet.5:6b).

It is only by the grace of God that one can maintain a humble attitude. Therefore, if you seek to be honoured, honour God by first submitting to Him. Jettison self-imposed honour and honour from men that do not have God's backing as they are short-lived.

Self-Imposed Honour

Self-imposed can be defined as something that you require or expect of yourself rather than something that is imposed on you by someone else because of your outstanding qualities. According to the above definition, self-imposed honour is that which you bestow on yourself without merit.

Typical example of self-imposed honour is recorded in the Bible (Dan.4:30-37) where the prideful King Nebuchadnezzar who thought he was entitled to honour by reason of his achievements met his "waterloo". He was deposed by God, abased as a beast and had to learn humility by force in the forest for seven (7) years before God had to restore him back to his kingdom with greater honour. Many of us are like Nebuchadnezzar; we try to impose honour on ourselves because of our elevated positions, chains of degree, wealth or endless number of achievements. Whatever strides you have made in the journey of life, keep your cool and work hard at counteracting the celebrity syndrome. For it is written in 2 Cor.10:18 (NLT):

> *When people commend themselves, it doesn't count much. The important thing is for the Lord to commend them.*

Not doing so will mean you want to take God's glory. Dare not try doing that for the story of the proud king in discussion was not a pleasant one for him, neither will it be for anyone who dares.

All honour, glory and power belong to God! Remember, Nebuchadnezzar was restored to his kingdom with greater honour because he saw himself as nothing before God after learning humility the hard way. Submitting himself to God, praising and honouring Him, Nebuchadnezzar earned for himself greater honour. Whoever honours God is honoured by God in return.

Honour from Men

All over the world, we see many politicians, presidents, traditional rulers, celebrities, and even ministers of the gospel seeking honour from men without realising that such honour is temporary and short-lived. In fact, giving lasting honour is the prerogative of God.

When men honour you because of your high status, popularity, wealth etc, that honour ends the moment you come down from that high position or cease to be in control of your domain of influence. I know many of such people who enjoyed men's honour while in their prominent positions but are no longer held in high esteem today because they have ceased to be relevant. However, few of those who honoured God while in their high positions are still relevant today and are honoured by God and men. Honour will never depart from those who honour God. One answer that readily comes to mind when the question of why men give honour to their fellow men is posed is that they do so because of what they hope to gain from such men of perceived honour.

When you find yourself in a position many people benefit from, your praise singers will increase, pretending to honour you. But when you are no longer in that position, the praise singers disappear, leaving no one left to honour you. King Nebuchadnezzar, from personal experience, can tell that story better. Therefore, is there any use in gloating or basking in the cooked-up honour of men? It is absolutely of no use to receive false honour from men. Rather, seek honour from God alone by honouring Him. What makes you think you deserve honour from men anyway? If you selfishly and solely think that only because of your achievements, men should honour you, you are making a big mistake because there is nothing you have that was not given to you by God. If not for God, you would not have been different from those from whom you seek honour. So let every man be subject to one another in humility, for God resists the proud and gives grace to the humble (1 Pet. 5:5).

Honour from God

Honour from God is dependent on the way you honour Him. Therefore, whoever desires honour must first of all honour God. Whatever your status is in life, you can be a man, woman, boy, or girl of honour provided you choose to love God and put Him first in all you do. Your high or low estate does not matter to God, but all that matters to Him is how you honour Him.

If only Haman in the Book of Esther Chapter 6 knew this, he would not have considered himself as the only man who deserved to be honoured when King Ahasuerus of Shushan asked for what should be done to the man the king desires to honour. Thinking honour was given through high position in office, popularity and being well connected, Haman enumerated what should be done to such a man in Esther 6:7-9 (KJV):

For the man whom the king delighted to honour,

Let the royal apparel be brought which the king useth to wear, and the horse that the king rideth upon and the crown royal which is set upon his head. And let this apparel and horse be delivered to the hand of one of the king's most noble princes, that they may array the man withal whom the king delighted to honour, and bring him on horse back through the street of the city, and proclaim before him, Thus shall it be done to the man the king delighted to honour.

To his greatest amazement and disappointment, Haman was asked to accord Mordecai (a Jewish gatekeeper) that honour, not missing out on anything. Why this turn of events? On a day the king had a sleepless night, it was discovered from the book of records read to the king that Mordecai unveiled the assassination plot by two (2) guards at his private quarters against him. When asked by the king what honour and dignity had been done to Mordecai, he was told nothing had been done for him. So the king decided to honour Mordecai himself. That is the way God will honour you, wherever you choose to honour Him. Every official in the king's palace bowed to honour Haman as the second in command to the king, but Mordecai refused to bow, as doing so would mean dishonouring his God whom Haman defied. It pays to honour God because He can cause people who looked down on you to honour you as in the case of Haman forcefully honouring Mordecai.

I enjoin readers of this book to shun self-imposed honour and honour from men. It does not pay; rather it ends in disgrace, embarrassment and destruction as in the scenario above. Seek unending honour by honouring God and humbling yourself before Him and your fellow men.

CHAPTER 5

TEST OF HUMILITY

If a personal opinion poll were to be used to ascertain the humility quotient of people, almost everyone, without considering the meaning of humility, would claim he or she is humble. But going by the simple Merriam-Webster definition of humility as "freedom from pride or arrogance: the quality or state of being humble", not many people can be said to be humble. In fact, the popular statement "My humble self" remains questionable and unacceptable until practically proven. A person's level of humility cannot be determined until he or she is tested in some way, which is difficult to do based solely on appearance or words. Practising humility is one of the hardest "nuts" to crack because it has to start with the recognition that you are not always right or have all the answers.

As a matter of fact, not many people pass the humility test easily. The very few who pass it easily do so by the grace of God in Christ that they have received. Short of this, there is false humility, which most people practise. We are living in a competitive world where one has to be aggressive to get what he or she wants in life, which, along with pride, is the opposite of humility.

True humility is to see ourselves as we actually are- fallen in sin and helpless without God. Seeing yourself in the light of the above helps you acknowledge God in all your ways for Him to direct your path (Proverbs 3:5). If you allow Him to direct your path, you can be sure you are on the path of true humility which entails doing the following:

1. **Value yourself and others:** Without recognition that you are no more or less important than others, you cannot come to terms with the fact that everyone has an equal right to be heard, or to listen to others. The test of true humility is our ability to listen to others. Spending time to listen to others, enabling them to be heard shows that you value people. The Samaritan woman at the well of Sychar in John 4:7-9 spent time listening to Jesus, even though the Samaritans had no dealings with the Jews as they probably felt they were more important. However, humbling herself to listen to Jesus revealed her emptiness, which led to her being filled. We are better off when we, in humility listen to

other people. But do we listen to others? This is the test of humility we must all strive to pass.

2. Be grateful for who you are and what you have: Godliness with contentment is great gain (1 Tim.6:6 KJV). The opposite of contentment is greed which drives one into many vices including pride. A proud person is never satisfied and will always want to make up for his or her shortfall in words (boasting) or action (showing off). If you are content with what you have, a competitive lifestyle will be far from you. You will not be envious or jealous of anyone; neither will you boast about who you are or what you have. You will just be yourself- calm and collected. Humility is found in the place of gratitude.

3. **Ask for help when you need it:** Nobody has it or knows it all. For you to think you have it or know it all shows you are proud and trying to compare yourself with God who knows and has everything (Psalm 24:1). The Sarophonician woman whose daughter was possessed by an evil spirit in (Mark 7:25-26 KJV) begged Jesus to cast out the demon from her daughter. Even when Jesus said that healing was his children's bread and not for dogs, she did not take offence that

she was referred to as a "dog" in the sense that she was not a Jew but a gentile. Rather she pleaded that even the dogs under the table are allowed to eat crumbs from the children's plate. It takes humility to beg to get what you want as seen in the case of this woman. Just as Jesus had declared, she went home and found her daughter healed. . When you swallow your pride and ask for help, help will come quickly. Are you still struggling with any issue in your life? There is always help very close by. Help can come from the least person you can ever imagine. Remember, help came to rescue Naman of his leprosy through a Jewish slave girl that served Naman's wife, according to 2 Kings 5:3 (NLT):

One day the girl said to her mistress. I wish my master would go to see the prophet in Samaria. He would heal him of his leprosy.

Just as help came to Naman, so shall it come your way if you choose not to look down on anyone like he did, initially.

4. **We gladly welcome constructive criticism:** Seek feedback from others on a regular basis as it is good to know what others think of you. People's evaluation of you will help you know how far or near you are

from humility. However, if you find it difficult to welcome criticism, then you are found wanting on the scale of humility. Humble people ensure that they are not misguided by their own abilities. Humility offers you the opportunity to become less self-involved and accommodate the feelings of other people. It appears to be self-defeating, though in the words of C.S. Lewis, "true humility is not thinking less of yourself, it is thinking of yourself less".

5. Appreciate others for their success: Have you ever wondered why many people are very quick to criticise other people for their failures but very slow at showing appreciation for their successes? It is perhaps because of the growing "selfishness" and "I" focus syndrome of the world. The feeling that "I am the best" and "no one can do it better than myself" has kept so many people from appreciating others for their successes. Being humble enough to appreciate people for their success, however, does not mean having a poor opinion of yourself. Rather, it means accepting yourself and your many good qualities, as well as your limitations, while taking cognizance of the fact that others also have good qualities and are also valuable.

6. **Be willing to serve others:** We live in a world where people prefer to be served than to serve. If everyone wants to be served, then there will be nobody to serve. Can you imagine what the world would have been like with masters without servants? The world would probably have come to a standstill just because service is lacking. On the other hand, people doubling as master and servant would be working it out themselves.

Oh! What a life of unproductivity and stress that would have been. But thank God that Jesus in His infinite wisdom gave us an example to follow in John 13:14-15 (KJV), with regards to serving others:

If I then, your Lord and Teacher, have washed your feet, you also ought to wash one another's feet, For I Have given you an example, that you should do as I have done.

Since Jesus, our Lord and Saviour—the greater than the greatest, the King of kings, and the Lord of lords—could stoop low to wash His disciples' feet, we ought to serve one another willingly. Serving others means recognising them and seeing them as valuable and worthy to serve and be served, simply because that is the way God sees them. Learn to love and serve others like Jesus. Indeed, much joy is derived from serving other people. Personally, I love to occasionally serve people who are paid to work for me. I cook and serve them and do chores within their scope, not just because they cannot cope with their work but because I value them and appreciate their services. Besides, the beam on their faces when I dare serve them gives me great joy and satisfaction. Halleluyah!

CHAPTER 6

HEROES OF HUMILITY

A hero is one who is admired by many people for his or her courage, outstanding qualities and great achievements. The mark of a true hero is humility. Many heroes of humility abound in the Bible and in our contemporary world to learn from. However, the few to be discussed in this chapter capture the very essential qualities of humility to emulate.

JESUS CHRIST- (The greatest HERO)
The first hero of humility, be it in the Bible or the contemporary world, is Jesus Christ—our Lord, our Saviour, and King of Kings. He is the perfect example of humility and remains the number one hero for all humanity. The height of Jesus' humility is recorded in Philippians 2:6-8 (KJV):

Who, being in the form of God, thought it not robbery to be equal with God: But made Himself of no reputation, and took upon him the form of a servant, and was made in the likeness of men: And being found in the fashion as a man, he humbled Himself and became obedient unto death, even the death of the cross.

The Triune God (The Father, Son, and Holy Spirit) sat in the majestic realms of heaven and reasoned: "Who will go and save man from sin?" Jesus, the son of God, out of His great love for us, chose to come in human form to die for our sins, knowing very well that the soul that sinneth must die. Not only did he come as a man, but he came, humbling himself as a servant, and died a painful and embarrassing death on the cross for the forgiveness of our sins and our total salvation. What an unthinkable act of showcasing humility, wherein divinity had to stoop down that low to identify with mere mortals for their rescue! In demonstrating such an incomparable height of humility, Jesus was lifted by God to the place of the highest honour and given a name that is above every other name (Phil. 2:9).

If you were to be Jesus, being God as well, could you have left your glorious estate to come to earth and be born of a virgin of low estate? No way! Considering the prideful nature of man, no earthly king, president, governor, CEO, or man or woman of repute could have done what Jesus did. Rather, they prefer to sit back and have people serve them with trepidation. Nevertheless, Jesus suffered and died for our sins because He is loving. It is said in 1 Cor. 13:4–7 (NLT) that:

> *Love is patient and kind. Love is not jealous or boastful or proud or rude. It does not demand its own way. It is not irritable, and it keeps no record of being wronged. It does not rejoice about injustice but rejoices whenever the truth wins out. Love never gives up, never loses faith, is always hopeful, and endures through every circumstance.*

His personality, as summed up in the above scripture, is without doubt and beyond reproach as a standard of humility for all to see and imitate. While Jesus walked this earth, He demonstrated humility in many ways:
- He was easily approachable by people generally.
- He was a friend of sinners i.e. tax collectors, and dined with them.
- He showed compassion to others- healing them and feeding them.
- He did not attribute the miracles He performed to Himself alone. He was a good team player—a "we" and

not an "I" person. Really, it takes God's kind of love to be humble.

Do you have love? Having love means loving God first, and loving God means giving up yourself to Him. When you do, you will receive love in return, and your lifestyle will be one of humility. Another example of humility worthy of note that Jesus left for us is in John 13:14–15 (KJV), where He washed the feet of His disciples, including Judas Iscariot, who betrayed him. It is written:

> If I then, your Lord and Master, have washed your feet; ye also ought to wash one another's feet. For I have given you an example that ye should do as I have done to you.

It is unimaginable that the King of Kings and Master of Masters had to wash the feet of His disciples, especially the one who betrayed Him.

Humanly speaking, it is the other way around, with the servant having to wash the feet of the master. But Jesus did this to teach us that we are all equal in the eyes of God and should serve one another. As we consider how Jesus took the place of entire subordination and gave God the honour and glory due to Him, let us strive to humble ourselves as we serve God and humanity. What a hero of humanity we have in Jesus. He is, without mincing words, my number one hero. What about you?

Moses

As herculean as the task of learning humility seems to all humans, the Bible singles out Moses as the meekest man on the face of the earth. Infact, it is unthinkable that a man raised as royalty, surrounded by all the luxuries of Egypt, a brash man and a murderer can be referred to as the most humble man on earth in the Bible in Numbers 12:3 (NLT):

Now Moses was very humble--more humble than any other person on earth.

How did Moses land here? Forty (40) years of herding sheep in the wilderness and encountering God in the burning bush must have helped the brash young Moses mature into a meek and humble man that could be used to bring the children of Israel out of their slavery in Egypt. In a similar vein, time and experience followed by a personal encounter with God, when handled appropriately, can work out patience and humility in us. Reading through the Bible, from Exodus to Deuteronomy, Moses demonstrated humility in many ways, from the time God called him for an assignment to the end of his life.

Following his personal encounter with God in the burning bush, Moses considered himself unfit for the assignment to go back to Egypt to deliver the children of Israel from their slavery. Remember, after killing an Egyptian who maltreated his fellow Jew, Moses fled Egypt for forty (40) years for fear of being killed by Pharaoh. How could God now be telling him to go back to the same man he was hiding from? In his helplessness, in Exodus 3:11 (NLT), he protested: "Who am I to appear before Pharaoh? Who am I to lead the people of Israel out of Egypt?" He probably thought there were better people than himself that God could send—obviously not an unworthy person like him. However, when God assured him of His backing, Moses obliged to go, with Aaron as his spokesman. He did not allow the authority he received to get into his head. Rather, he trusted in God with all his heart, leaning not on his own understanding but on God to carry out that seemingly impossible task.

The humility of Moses can be said to be a type and shadow of the humility of Jesus Christ. This is because in all of life's circumstances, he put God first, then the needs of others, and lastly, his own comfort and preferences. While putting God first, Moses never did anything without getting instructions from God and following such instructions, except in one instance of having to strike the rock instead of speaking to it for water to come out for his people to drink. He did this, however, because he was so angry with them for their ingratitude for all the signs and wonders wrought by God to rescue them from the Egyptian bonds. Oh! How consumed he must have been by the zeal of the Lord! Read this record from Numbers 20:1-13. In his dealings with the people, Moses demonstrated humility beyond human imagination. Just like Jesus, he took insults and humiliation from those he accepted to help them gain their freedom from slavery. When efforts seemed to prove abortive, seeing that the Egyptians were overtaking them, the people yelled at him, complaining, as seen in Exodus 14:11-12 (NLT):

Why did you bring us out here to die in the wilderness? Weren't there enough graves for us in Egypt? What have you done to us? Why did you make us leave Egypt? Didn't we tell you this would happen while we were still in Egypt? We said, Leave us alone! Let us be slaves to the Egyptians. It is better to be a slave in Egypt than a corpse in the wilderness!

How did Moses react when his brethren or the Israelites went into such a tantrum? It will surprise you to know that he was not angry with them. Rather, he was patient enough to stand by them and encourage them thus:

Don't be afraid. Just stand still and watch the Lord rescue you today. The Egyptians you see today will never be seen again. The Lord himself will fight for you. Just stay calm (Ex.14:13-14 NLT).

How many people can take insults from those they are trying to help? It is very rare to come across such a person. It takes one with the mind of Christ, like Moses, to take insults from people and still go ahead and help them. In fact, each time the people complained and turned against Moses for one challenge or another in the wilderness, he did not retaliate but simply cried to God for help. I don't know how many people would have been that patient.

Is it when the water was bitter and not good for drinking and they turned against him? Is it when there was no food or when at Rephidim (Exodus 17:1), where there was no water for the people to drink and they wanted to stone him? In all these circumstances, Moses did not retaliate but cried to God for help at each turn. Again, Moses as a leader demonstrated humility in his willingness to accept his father-in-law's advice in his administration of justice to his people. Do you care to listen to others? Or do you think you know it all, especially as a leader? Moses was humble enough to reason with Jethro (his father-in-law), and seeing his flaws, he followed his suggestion to appoint capable men as leaders over the people to settle their common disputes. The work was made easier as only the major cases were brought to him to settle.

Thank God he listened to good counsel; otherwise, he would have worked himself to an untimely death. Many who are not humble enough to take advice from wiser and more experienced people don't live long, but Moses, due to his humble disposition, lived up to one hundred and twenty (120) years. Therefore, be humble if you desire riches, honour, and a long life (Proverbs 22:4).

Really, the whole life of Moses was laced with humility. In Numbers 11:29, when Eldad and Medad prophesied in the camp and Joshua asked Moses to stop them, his reply was that he wished all the Lord's people were prophets with God's spirit upon them. As a man or woman of God, do you appreciate the gift of God in the lives of members to get them involved? Or you enjoy being the only one to be seen and heard. If you are humble, you will always give others a chance to be heard.

In Numbers 27:1-11, Moses gave the daughters of Zelophehad a fair hearing when they presented an inheritance petition to him, saying in Numbers 27:7 (NLT):

> *The claim of the daughters of Zelophehad is legitimate. You must give them a grant of land along with their father's relatives. Assign them the property that would have been given to their father.*

This singular act resulted in a change in the inheritance law in Israel, whereby the daughters of a man who died without a son were to inherit their father's property.

The humility demonstrated by Moses in his dealing with his siblings (Aaron and Miriam) is worthy of note. When they criticized him for marrying an Ethiopian Woman and questioned his authority in Num. 12:2 (NLT) saying:

"Has the Lord spoken only through Moses? Hasn't He spoken through us too?"

He said nothing, but God reacted in anger, saying in Num. 12:6-8 (NLT):
If there were prophets among you, I the Lord, would reveal myself in visions. I would speak to them in dreams. But not with my servant Moses. I speak to him face to face, clearly, and not in riddles! He sees the Lord as He is so why were you not afraid to criticize my servant Moses?

Immediately after God finished talking and left, Mariam became leprous. When Mariam incurred the wrath of God, Moses rather than say: "It serves her right", cried out to God to heal her.

Furthermore, when the people rebelled against God and worshipped idols at the time he was on the mountain to receive the Ten Commandments and God, in his hot displeasure, was to destroy them, Moses pleaded with God to pacify Him. He was not selfish; otherwise, he would have jumped at God's offer to destroy them and make a greater nation out of him. He even went to the extent of pleading with God to forgive their sins, stressing that if God does not forgive their sins, He should erase his name from his book of records.

But now, if you will only forgive their sin- but if not, erase my name from the record you have written (Ex.32:32 NLT).

This kind of humility is similar to that of Jesus, who cared nothing about himself to the point of dying a shameful death to save us from our sins. Moses was vested with so much power by reason of his unique relationship with God that his brethren could hardly behold his face without a veil. Yet he always showed restraint out of his love for them. If he chose to use the power vested in him to discipline them, he could have. But for humility's sake, he did not. What a hero of humility to emulate!

Dear reader, you can also seek this kind of humility. What this means is that you must consider others better than yourself and look out for their interests. Live a life of God first, then others, and yourself last.

Paul

The list of heroes of humility in the Bible will be incomplete without the mention of Apostle Paul. This is a man, going by his early life and antecedents had become a colossus to all eyes in various spheres of life. His resume recorded in Phil.3:4-6 (NLT) is an allusion to that:

Though I could have confidence in my own effort if anyone could. Indeed, if others have reason for confidence in their own efforts, I have even more! I was circumcised when I was eight days old. I am a pure-blooded citizen of Israel and a member of the Pharisees, who demand the strictest obedience to the Jewish law. I was so zealous that I harshly persecuted the church. And as for righteousness I obeyed the law without fault.

However, from the time Paul had a dramatic encounter with Christ and was transformed from Saul (the murderous persecutor of Christ followers) to Paul, the self in him died. He became so selfless that despite his achievements in kingdom matters, he was never puffed up but attributed all his efforts to God, saying in 1 Cor. 15:9-10 (NLT):

For I am the least of all the apostles. Infact, I'm not even worthy to be called an apostle after the way I persecuted God's church. But whatever I am now, it is all because God poured out His special favour on me- and not without results. For I have worked harder than any of the apostles; yet it was not I but God who was working through me by His grace.

Like Paul, can we really say that we are what we are now because of the grace of God upon our lives? If we all do, the man of God who takes pride in his anointing will not have his picture on his crusade banner with the writing, "Bishop X or Apostle Z storms the town". He would rather have the picture of Jesus with the writing, Jesus storms the town. The politicians will not boastfully claim they are the ones empowering the citizenry as they do, forgetting they are using government funds and not theirs. You hear them say, "I have done this or that," as if they do whatever they do with their own money. Why act so proudly? Don't you know that no condition is permanent? It is God who puts or removes one from office. Paul realised this and chose to live the rest of his life after his encounter with God in humility.

In humility, Paul lived a life of contentment. Not minding that he was an accomplished lawyer, he became a tentmaker in order not to be a burden to the Philippian brethren. In Phil. 4:11-12 (NLT), he stated:

Not that I was ever in need, for I have learned how to be content with whatever I have. I know how to live on almost nothing or with everything. I have learnt the secret of living in every situation, whether it is with a full stomach or empty, with plenty or little.

Are you a man or woman of God? Take a cue from the life of Paul and do whatever work you can do to take care of yourself and also support the work of God. Do not feel too big as "Papa" or "Mama", "Bishop" or "Archbishop" to work, even when it is so glaring that your congregation is struggling to meet your welfare and other needs of the church. Paul served the Lord with all humility and suffered for the gospel's sake. He endured shipwrecks, beatings, imprisonments, earthquakes, and persecutions simply because all he ever thought was valuable; he considered such to be worthless when compared with the infinite value of knowing Jesus Christ (Phil. 3:8 NLT). When you have Jesus, nothing else will matter to you. You will cease to be involved with the rat race where everyone wants to be seen and heard. Unfortunately, many are caught up in the web of this competitive lifestyle because they value the things of this world more than Jesus, the author of salvation. As for me, it is a high mark of humility to let go of who you were and become who God made you to be. Although Paul was such a legendary figure, he became all things to all men. He became a slave (servant) to all people to bring many to Christ (1 Cor. 9:19 NLT). No wonder he said, "For me to live is Christ, and to die is gain" (Phil.1:21).

What are you living for? Are you living for wealth, degrees, power, fame etc? Remember, all is vanity. So even when you have these things, keep your cool, pricing Jesus above them. For it's only when you have Jesus that you gain when you die.

Ruth

Also worthy of note on the list of heroes of humility is Ruth the Moabite. This young lady, who followed her mother-in-law, Naomi, back to Bethlehem despite all entreaties for her to return to her people while she (Naomi) left, demonstrated humility beyond human comprehension. There was absolutely no reason for her to go with Naomi, who had lost her husband, and her two sons, of whom one (Kilion) was Ruth's husband.

Life was bitter for Naomi, and having to leave Moab in a state of hopelessness, she did not see any reason why Ruth, her daughter-in-law, should go back home with her. But Ruth, having learned much about the God of Naomi, the Almighty God (God of Abraham, Isaac, and Jacob), vowed never to part with her. She was determined to go with Naomi against all odds for compassion's sake and also because of her love for the God of Israel, as seen in Ruth 1:16-17 (NLT):

> *But Ruth replied, don't ask me to leave you and turn back. Wherever you go, I will go; wherever you live, I will live. Your people will be my people, and your God will be my God. Wherever you die, I will die, and there I will be buried. May the Lord punish me severely if I allow anything but death to separate us.*

Wow! What would have made a young girl like Ruth take such a decision instead of going back to her people, remarrying, and having a new beginning? She probably considered that doing that would mean starting all over without the living God—the God of wonders—as her people did not know that God. She was prepared to go even if it meant suffering to make ends meet, provided the God of Naomi was her God. Really, it takes a broken, compassionate, and humble person to do what Ruth did. Generally, people go for the greener pasture, not the other way around—the way of Ruth. As a broken, compassionate, and humble person, it was easy for Ruth to show kindness to Naomi and serve her faithfully. How many young women in our present world care about their mother-in-laws who are well off, much less those who are struggling to survive like Naomi? I guess very few; many are in competition or on a warpath with their mothers-in-law. To earn a living and fend for herself and her mother-in-law, Ruth opted for a menial job. She said to Naomi in Ruth 2:2b (NLT): "Let me go out into the harvest fields to pick up the stalks of grain left behind by anyone who is kind enough to let me do it". Approval was granted, and off she went, unknown to her, to gather grain behind the harvesters in a field that belonged to Boaz, the relative of her father-in-law, Elimelech. Quite interesting! God indeed orders the steps of the righteous. Ruth found favour in the sight of Boaz and was told by him to always glean in his fields, for she had dealt well with Naomi since she (Ruth) lost her husband.

In humility, she fell at his feet and thanked him, saying in Ruth 2:10b (NLT): "What have I done to deserve such kindness? "I am only a foreigner". Humility goes with gratitude. Knowing where she is coming from and accepting her present condition, she cannot help but appreciate the one who has begun making a difference in her life. Do you care to appreciate people that help you? It pays to do so, for that will open more doors of favour for you. In Ruth 2:14 (NLT), Boaz continued to show Ruth kindness:

> *At mealtime, Boaz called to her, come over here, and help yourself to some food. You can dip your bread in the sour wine. So she sat with his harvesters, and Boaz gave her some roasted grain to eat. She ate all she wanted and had some left over.*

Showing gratitude earned Ruth acceptance, as seen in the invitation extended to her by Boaz to dine with him and his harvesters. Not only was she invited to dine with them, but an order was given by Boaz to the harvesters to deliberately drop some grains for her to pick. As a result, she went home with a filled basket, which she presented to her mother-in-law. In addition, she gave her the leftovers of her meal. What a hardworking, caring, and compassionate lady!

Are you a daughter reading this book? I urge you to make Ruth your hero and emulate her. Care for your mother-in-law, your mother, and everyone that crosses your path. Be humble to receive wise counsel. Ruth followed Naomi's counsel on how to woo Boaz, knowing he was such a close kinsman. Eventually, as the next family redeemer, he married her since the first one had declined.

Ruth won Boaz's heart as a result of her humility and other virtues. To Boaz, she was a virtuous woman (Ruth 3:11b NLT). It pays to be humble, as we can see in the life of Ruth. Her humility paid off because, being married to Boaz, she became a major part of Israel's story, an ancestor of King David and Jesus Christ. Everything ended well for Ruth just because she denied herself, remained faithful, and humbly accepted her position.

Nelson Mandela

Talking about heroes of humility in our contemporary world, the name Nelson Mandela readily comes to mind as it resonates across the globe. To this end, the South African anti-apartheid revolutionary and Nobel Peace Prize winner is undoubtedly humility personified. On her show in 2000, Oprah Winfrey said Nelson Mandela was the most humble man she had ever met. While speaking with him in an interview, he said, "Humility is one of the most important qualities you must have. If you are humble, if you make people realise that you are no threat to them, then people will embrace you and they will listen to you". True to his statement, Mandela, by reason of his humility, was one person the whole world revered and always wanted to listen to. No wonder, he won the mandate of his people shortly after his twenty-seven (27) year imprisonment to be the first democratically elected black president of South Africa from 1994 to 1999—a position he never allowed to get into his head.

As a leader, he demonstrated uncommon humility by declaring publicly his forgiveness for those who imprisoned him for 27 years and maltreated him, his family, and the South African people. Instead of taking vengeance on them, he opted for peaceful coexistence. This is a lesson for all, especially leaders in various capacities. When people attain great feats, it is natural to become high-minded. But with Mandela, the reverse was the case, as he opted for only a single term of five (5) years in office. In fact, he opted out of a second term, contrary to the practise of African leaders who hold on to power as if it were personal property.

Handing over power voluntarily just after one tenure of office is unimaginable in today's competitive world, where people are power drunk and strive to stand out at all costs. Nevertheless, Mandela's belief in the importance of an all-inclusive South Africa compelled him to give another person a chance. What a rare act of selflessness! More on his rare show of humility is in an article by Pippa Green.

According to Pippa Green, Mandela saw the honorary doctorate award from Harvard at a special convocation in 1998 not as his personal achievement but rather as a tribute paid to the struggles and achievements of the South African people as a whole. He further said: "To join George Washington and Winston Churchill as the other recipients of such an award conferred at a specially convened convocation is not only a singular honour." It also holds great symbolic significance to the mind and to the future memory of this American institution; the name of an African is now added to those two illustrious leaders of the Western world".

This is a rare show of humility: a politician desiring to be seen as not separate from his organisation, the African National Congress. A man who is not carried away by the honour done to him but by that which is done to an Africa, and to Africa as a whole. The humility of Nelson Mandela can never be overemphasised. His personality, speech, and appearance always had a humble undertone. He wore the trademarked Mark Batik shirts buttoned to the collar as formal dressing and got away with it, as it soon became a trending fashion for the world. Wow! Coming from a revered world icon who saw himself as ordinary, it must be fashionable—an affirmation of one of his quotes that there is nothing to popularise a man but humility. On his death, encomiums by people who had personal encounters with him—from political leaders to people of all climes and strata—published in the world's media as well as speeches at his funeral revealed his outstanding humility. Humility and power are a rare combination, but Mandela showed them both in life and death.

What about you, dear reader? Do you treat people with respect simply because they are human beings just like you? Do you acknowledge that there are things you do not know and that you can learn from others, even if their ideas differ from yours? Do you accept being wrong or that someone else's view might be better than yours?

Nelson Mandela, indeed, is one person who lived a life of positive affirmation to the forgone questions. What a hero to emulate!

Another hero of humility as I end this chapter is the one I have known for over forty (40) years out of the six (6) decades of my existence. Though coming from a privileged background, he chose to identify with his mother when things became tough for his family after the death of his father. In his teenage years and into early adulthood, he stooped low to conquer. Many children with similar stories today, out of pride, refuse to adapt to the current situation they find themselves in. Some have fled their homes and are hanging out with friends and relatives who are well off. Others, however, have taken to criminality, with some lasting a long time. But this hero stuck with his family against all odds, making sacrifices throughout his early life journey to become who he is today. What the Bible says about humility preceding honour in Prov. 18:12b is real in the life of this amazing hero, who by the grace of God happens to be my husband, Orok. This hero exudes humility wherever he finds himself. At home, he demonstrates uncommon humility while dealing with every family member. He is always patient enough to listen to my views and act on those he considers more reasonable than his.

Not many men do this in a male-dominance domain as dominant as ours. He is always quick to apologise when he goes wrong. Quick to say thank you in appreciation for whatever service I render as a wife, even though it is my responsibility to do so. He knows when I am tired from housework and often helps out with the menial housework, such as cleaning the toilets! As a father, grandfather, and father-in-law, he is easily accessible and often comes down to the level of all the children, grandchildren, and in-laws, making them feel at home with his high sense of humour. With him, there is no dull moment. When he was in service, not minding his position as a top management staff member, he related freely with members of staff much more below his level. Even secretaries, messengers, drivers, and cleaners were very free with him, as he often engaged them in jokes to relax them at work.

To many in society, he is an enigma because of his

humility. When many call him "chief" a title he is not interested in holding, and he refutes them, they say to him, "You have done much more than those who claim to be chiefs or high chiefs". In church, he is humility par excellence, one of the few Knights who attend Bible studies and prayer meetings in his local church. He is a peacemaker and a great unifier. However, in trying to build the church, what he gets at times is insult. But by reason of his love for Jesus, he is ever ready to keep serving in humility. After all, if Jesus did not mind all the insults and shame to the extent of dying for us, we too should humble ourselves before God and man no matter what happens.

It pays to be humble, just as we have seen in the lives of the heroes of humility mentioned in this chapter. Dear reader, to easily emulate the humility of these heroes, you have to surrender your life to Jesus—our perfect example of humility. Other than this, you cannot demonstrate true humility.

CHAPTER 7

LANGUAGE OF HUMILITY

Language is a means of human communication, be it by speech, writing or gesture. By this definition, we have verbal, written and body language through which we communicate with each other, some of which show our pride or humility. Since humility is the state of not thinking you are better than other people, love is therefore, the language of humility.

According to 1 Cor. 13:4-5 (NLT):
Love is patient and kind. Love is not jealous or boastful or proud or rude. It does not demand its own way. It is not irritable, and it keeps no record of being wrong.

From the scripture above, it is certain that without love, we will find it difficult to express humility, be it in speech, writing or gesture. However, if we have love for each other, doing so becomes easy in every circumstance as mentioned below.

When We Hurt People

Because we are different from each other and unique in our ways of doing things, we are bound to hurt one another in some way or another. When you hurt someone, what do you do? To show that you are humble, the first thing you say is "I am sorry". That being said, rather than say "I am sorry," many give excuses to justify their actions. A proud person does not see any reason why he or she should apologise for being wrong, as he or she always claims to be right. Nevertheless, if people could just say "I am sorry", the frictions we have in marriages, offices, schools, churches, nations, and the world at large would not exist. For example, my husband and I have stuck together in marriage for 42 years because, by the grace of God, we have been speaking this language of humility—I am sorry—to each other whenever offence comes. In any case, why should such a short phrase as this be such a bitter pill for people to swallow? It beats my imagination, but it is most probably because people lack love, which the Bible says is not proud. When you love, you will not be puffed up to apologise and ask for forgiveness.

When we make Mistakes

It is often said that it is human to err, but divine to

forgive. This means we are all prone to making mistakes and, as such, should take responsibility for our actions. Although we all agree that man is fallible and only God is infallible, it takes courage to admit your mistakes and take responsibility for your wrong actions. However, if you are humble, doing so comes easily because you do not demand your own way. Also, you will not allow shame to hinder you from taking responsibility because you know doing that will not change who you are but rather add to your worth. Some people don't like taking responsibility for their actions for fear of the repercussions of their actions. Even if we face adverse consequences for taking responsibility for our actions, it is nonetheless beneficial as it offers us a chance to correct our mistakes. When we correct ourselves, we develop ourselves as we learn new things.

I remember one occasion when my tailor made a mistake in sewing a gown I designed for him. When I went to pick up my gown, it was a different design from the one I wanted. When I pointed it out, he owned up to his mistake and followed the instructions I gave him to make the gown fine and unique. In fact, that gown is now one of my most fitting gowns, and the tailor himself was happy to have learned a new and unique design. When we correct ourselves, we develop ourselves as we learn new things. Until you accept responsibility for your actions or failures, it will be quite difficult for you to develop self-respect or even have the respect of others.

A humble person takes responsibility for any error committed. He or she will not shift blame onto other vulnerable people but will readily own up to his or her mistakes, saying, "I take responsibility". As a husband, do you shift blame onto your wife? Wife, what about you? Do you shift blame onto your husband, children, and carers? If you do, you better stop and start taking up your responsibility, or else you will lower your self-respect with your integrity at stake.

When we See People in Need

We are living in a world of inequality. Some people are more privileged than others. When you see somebody less privileged than you who is in need of one thing or another, what do you do? Your response will depend on whether you are humble or proud. If you are humble, you will give the person food and clothes if that is his or her need, and if he or she is lonely and needs company, you will visit him or her. But a proud person, not wanting to be associated with people of lower status than him or her, will simply walk by, pretending not to be aware of such needs.

It takes humility to be able to care in order to make a difference in the life of another person. Always willing to help, a humble person helps those in need without accepting anything in return, be it recognition or a thank you. My husband and I take pleasure in helping people who cannot repay us in any way. What really matters to us is that God is blessing us for making a difference in the lives of people in our own little way.

Really, it pays to help people, be it in your family, place of work, church, or community. When you do so without strings attached, the blessings of God will overtake you. But when you do it for recognition, fame, or power like the politicians, you are no longer speaking the language of humility in that gesture.

When we see people's Achievement

How we react when we see people succeed in any area of their lives speaks volumes about our level of humility. Achievers around us deserve our commendations and accolades, but the phrases "well done", and congratulations, sir or madam, are being hoarded and rarely heard in our daily interactions with people. The proud find it difficult to rejoice with those who succeed at anything because he or she does not want praise to go to people other than himself or herself. With the humble, the reverse is true, as he or she values others as much as himself or herself. Avoiding competition, you hear the humble say "Well done", "I am proud of you" and Congratulations, sir or ma."

I remember many years ago that my neighbour, rather than congratulate my husband and me when she saw the BMW car we just bought in our garage, said she wondered why she was not also getting money to buy a car. To her, she deserved to own that car—not us!

When you succeed as a team

As a leader of any group, it is expected of you to see the group's success as success for everybody in that group and not just yours. However, if you are not a humble person, you will not be able to say "We did it". You will rather say "I did it". We hear this very often as we listen to proud leaders recount their achievements in office. They fail to appreciate other team members because they do not want them to also bask in that success. They will probably think, "Far be it that others should take credit for this achievement. I should take all the credit as the boss, so that I will be the only one to be honoured." A humble person will not act in this manner. He will think of others before himself instead of drawing attention to himself alone. Are you carrying your team members along by projecting them in your success story? Man of God, woman of God, who takes the credit for the growth of your church? If you fail to give every member of your church credit for that, then you lack the language of humility.

When people do good to you

Any time I hear the statement, "I am a self-made man or woman", I wonder if that person making such a statement is an island. I believe you are where you are today because somebody supported you in some way. The support may have come in the form of counselling, training, financial support, and moral support, to name just a few. In whichever way you get help from somebody, the onus is on you to acknowledge that person, appreciate him or her, and thank him or her. Responding in this way will show you are humble and understand the language of humility. A few years ago, my husband and I attended the funeral of someone my late father-in-law nurtured in his home while growing up, only to discover that there was no mention at all of that support in his biography. His children carefully glossed over that aspect of their father's life because they painted a picture of their father as a self-made "Prince". Oh! They lacked the language of humility because they chose to act proudly.

What about you? Do you appreciate people's good gestures towards you? How well you talk about such people will show that you accept yourself as you are, pointing to the fact that you are a humble person.

Besides the afore-mentioned circumstances wherein we can express humility, there are other situations that require our show of humility. For instance, it is expected of us to greet our seniors when we see them, give up our seats for them where they have none, and pay people compliments for their good dress sense, presentations, cooking, and services. All these and many more will expand your vocabulary in the language of humility.

Conclusion

Gleaning from all that has been written about humility in this book, one thing to go home with is that being humble does not mean you should think less of yourself or that others are better than you. But what it really means is that you should not consider yourself more important than other people. With this mindset, you should value yourself and other people as well. Have respect for yourself and others. Do not let people trample on you as a doormat because you are not one.

Finally, be open to learning and live humbly in any situation you find yourself in, for by doing so, you will be building up your character, perspective, and vision, which will make you a force to be reckoned with. As you complete reading this work, my earnest prayer for you is that you will ascend to higher levels in the school of humility! Bravo!!

REFERENCES

Fickett, Harold: Faith that works G/L Regal Books, (1972)

Green, Pippa: Pippa Green@green_Pippa, (2013)

Mata, Amritanandamayi. Quote on Humility. Quote Master. Org.

Mandela, Nelson. A-Z Quotes

Winfrey, Oprah. Interview with Nelson Mandela, (2000)

A Brief Profile of Ubong Orok Ekpenyong

Dr (Mrs) Ubong Orok Ekpenyong is an Educationist. She has a Ph.D in Social Studies Education. Her greatest desire is to see people serve God and man in integrity and total humility. She is an intercessor, marriage counsellor, preacher and doer of the word by God's grace.

Ubong Ekpenyong and her husband have been married for 43 years and are blessed with 4 children and 8 grand children. She lives with her husband in Port Harcourt, Rivers state, Nigeria.

www.ingramcontent.com/pod-product-compliance
Lightning Source LLC
Chambersburg PA
CBHW050308120526
44590CB00016B/2536